© Aladdin Books Ltd 1989

Designed and produced by
Aladdin Books Ltd
70 Old Compton Street
London W1

Design   David West
              Children's Book Design
Editorial Planning   Clark Robinson Limited
Editor   Bibby Whittaker
Researcher   Cecilia Weston-Baker
Illustrated by   Ron Hayward Associates
                      and Simon Bishop

EDITORIAL PANEL
The author, Hugh Johnstone,
is an engineer and
science writer who
specializes in transport.

The educational consultant, Peter
Thwaites, is Head of Geography at
Windlesham House School in
Sussex.

The editorial consultant, John Clark,
has contributed to many
information and reference books.

First published in the
United States in 1989 by
Gloucester Press
387 Park Avenue South
New York, NY 10016

Printed in Belgium

Library of Congress Cataloging-in-Publication Data

Johnstone, Hugh,
      Land and sea transports   by Hugh Johnstone.
         p.   cm. – (Today's World)
      Includes index.
      Summary: Describes, in text and illustrations, the characteristics
and functions of a variety of land and sea vehicles including
barges, hydrofoils, trucks, automobiles, and high-speed trains.
      ISBN 0-531-17186-8
      1. Vehicles – Juvenile literature.   2. Ships – Juvenile literature.
[1. Vehicles.   2. Ships.]   I. Title.   II. Series.
TL147.J64   1989
629.04–dc20
                                                                89-31562
                                                                CIP
                                                                AC

TODAY'S WORLD

LAND AND SEA TRANSPORT

HUGH JOHNSTONE

GLOUCESTER PRESS
New York · London · Toronto · Sydney

CONTENTS

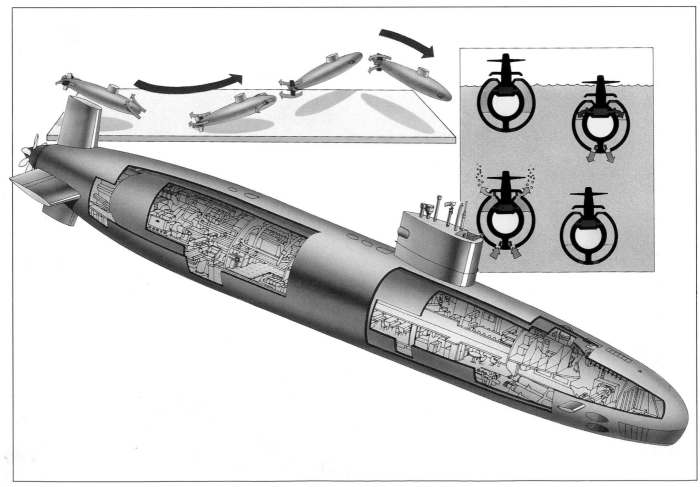

The front cover photograph shows a modern container ship.

INTRODUCTION

A world without land and sea transport would be unimaginable, it is such a part of our daily lives. Many people choose to travel by car, motorcycle or bicycle. Although this allows freedom of travel, it can create massive traffic congestion in and around big cities. Efficient public transport systems are continually being improved to offer alternative travel. Rail transport includes fast intercity services, short commuter services – both overground and underground – and cable cars. Buses can be operated efficiently in regional areas or in high-density traffic. Although everyday travel for most people involves transport on land, passengers also use waterborne transport in the form of ferries, hovercraft and passenger liners.

The movement of freight often involves more than one form of transport. Trucks vary from small delivery vehicles, to huge oil tankers and long-distance juggernauts, and they often collect and deliver goods that have come by sea or rail. Ships themselves range from barges and small coastal freighters, to large container ships and supertankers.

An empty supertanker rides high in the water, revealing its bulbous hull

BOATS AND SHIPS

In 1952, the *United States* made the fastest Atlantic crossing by liner in 3 days, 10 hours and 40 minutes.

Supertankers are the biggest ships in the world. Some are up to 450 m (1,500 ft) long and can carry more than 550,000 tons of crude oil.

In 1960 the manned bathyscape *Trieste* reached a record depth of 10,917 m (35,820 ft) in the Pacific Mariana Trench.

Boats and ships come in all shapes and sizes for different purposes. Sea transport is the main way of moving heavy and bulky freight from country to country, either across oceans or using inland waterways. Many ships are built as all-purpose bulk carriers, but oil and gas tankers, container ships and car ferries are designed for their specific cargos. Other boats are used purely for fun, from large ocean-going leisure yachts to small sailing dinghies.

In an age when air travel is fast and relatively inexpensive, passenger services by sea are now concentrated on the holiday cruise lines and short-haul ferry journeys, for which fast superferries, hydrofoils and hovercraft provide efficient short-distance transportation. And all vessels, from a supertanker to a pleasure yacht, rely on a port, harbor, marina or simple mooring from which to operate.

The busy port

Ships and boats rely on the efficiency of services offered by a harbor system. As soon as an ocean-going vessel is maneuvered by tugs to its berth, dock workers unload and reload the ship. Refueling, replenishing supplies and some simple repairs may also have to be carried out.

Key

1 Heavy lift ship	10 Lightship
2 Gas tanker	11 Tugboat
3 Submarine	12 Hydrofoil
4 Aircraft carrier	13 Grain ship
5 Sail-assisted cargo ship	14 Cruise liner
6 Hovercraft	15 Fishing boats
7 Ro-Ro ferry	16 Lifeboat
8 Barge	17 Pleasure craft (yachts and motorboats)
9 Container ship	

Propulsion

Oars and paddles are the simplest form of propulsion and a rowing eight can reach a speed of nearly 22 km/h (14 mph). Sails use the power of the wind and for centuries have been used to drive all types of craft. Clipper ships – designed to carry light cargo (originally tea) – achieved speeds of up to 37 km/h (23 mph), while modern racing yachts can exceed 65 km/h (41 mph).

Early steam ships used paddle wheels, because they were easier to make and more reliable than the first propellers. Propellers have a screw-like action. Driven by a steam engine, diesel engine or nuclear-powered steam turbine, they thrust against the water to push the ship forward. A single propeller of a giant supertanker may be nearly 6 m (20 ft) across and weigh more than 30 tonnes.

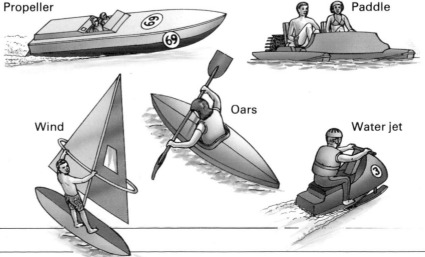

Propeller

Paddle

Wind

Oars

Water jet

TYPES AND DESIGN

A large modern container ship can carry at least 2,000 18-ton containers.

SRN4 hovercraft ferries carry 418 passengers and 60 vehicles at over 110 km/h (70 mph).

The weight of a ship is evenly supported by the water, and at slow speeds the main resistance to motion is drag due to water moving over the hull surface. This is comparatively small so ships move easily even when heavily loaded, making them very good for transporting large loads that can be moved slowly. But drag increases rapidly with speed, so that a lot more power is needed to move the ship and increase speed. This effect limits most modern cargo ships to cruising speeds of 20 to 35 km/h (12-22 mph). High-speed vessels have hulls designed to minimize drag.

Hull design

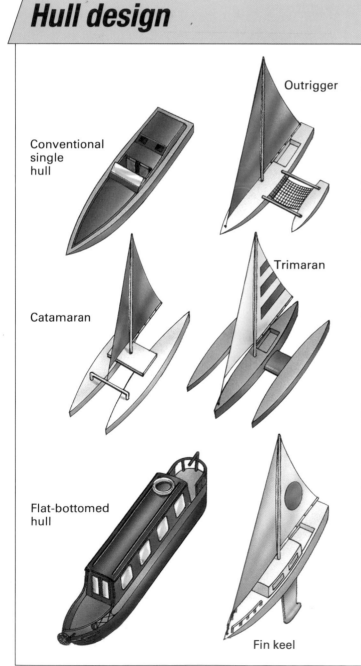

Conventional single hull

Outrigger

Catamaran

Trimaran

Flat-bottomed hull

Fin keel

The hull is the main body of the ship. Early small vessels, such as canoes, had long narrow hulls and often needed an outrigger to prevent them from capsizing (overturning). Speedboats have dart-shaped hulls to cut through the water.

On most commercial cargo vessels the hull has square sides, curving around to a virtually flat bottom and tapering to the bows and stern. Hulls of this type are stable, have good carrying capacity, and are reasonably easy to drive through the water. Large ships often have a bulbous projection at the bow; this improves the water flow around the hull and reduces drag.

The keel is the lowest section of the hull running the whole length of the vessel. On sailing yachts the keel may extend below the main body of the hull and be made of a heavy material such as cast iron to give stability.

A fishing boat with a broad, stable hull

Containers and barges

Most general cargo is transported in standard metal containers which arrive pre-packed at the docks and are loaded directly onto the ship by a special crane. Aboard ship the containers fit into angled steel guides in the hold or are locked together into stacks up to four high as deck cargo. Standard containers have a capacity of 36 cubic metres (1,280 cu ft) and can hold about 18 tons.

Another system uses lighters, or barges, which are loaded with 500 tons of cargo, towed into the open stern of a special LASH (Lighter Aboard Ship) ship and hoisted onto the deck. Another system uses larger barges that can carry up to 2,000 tons. The ship then makes an ocean crossing to its destination. At the end of the journey the barges are lowered back into the water and towed off to their final destination by small tugs. Barges also carry freight on inland waterways such as lakes, rivers and canals.

Crane for loading ships

A barge carrying a bulk cargo

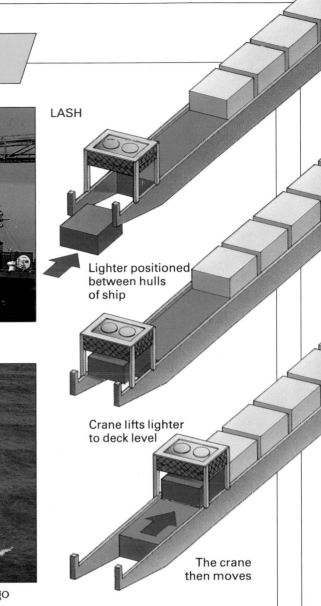
LASH

Lighter positioned between hulls of ship

Crane lifts lighter to deck level

The crane then moves

Tankers and grain ships

Some cargos, such as grain, coal and metal ores, are best carried in bulk. The ship's cargo space is divided into a series of separate holds and the loose material poured in. Unloading is by grab buckets, suction pipes or elevator systems and some are equipped to unload their own cargos without the need for port facilities. Oil is a major bulk cargo transported throughout the world in tankers. Fuel gases are refrigerated to liquify them for carrying in insulated tanks.

A grain ship being unloaded by suction pipes

LNG tanker

Crude oil tanker

Passenger ships and ferries

There are two main types of passenger vessels: cruise liners and ferries. Cruise liners are really floating hotels with up to 600 cabins for private bedrooms. There are also bars, restaurants, nightclubs, movie theaters and shops to keep the passengers occupied on leisure voyages.

Vehicle ferries have large doors at one or both ends so that cars, trucks and buses can be driven on and off. Ro-Ro (standing for roll-on roll-off) ships may also have ramps for easy loading of vehicles on two decks. The ferries have seating and restaurants for drivers and their passengers, and vessels on longer routes have sleeping cabins. High-speed ferries generally use air-cushion vehicles – hovercraft – or hydrofoils. Vosper HM527 hovercraft ferries operating in Hong Kong can carry 200 passengers at a cruising speed of 66 km/h (41 mph). Hydrofoils have under-hull "wings" that lift the hull clear of the water at speed. Sea-going designs have a similar performance to hovercraft ferries.

A hovercraft used as a car ferry

A Ro-Ro ferry with upward-hinging doors

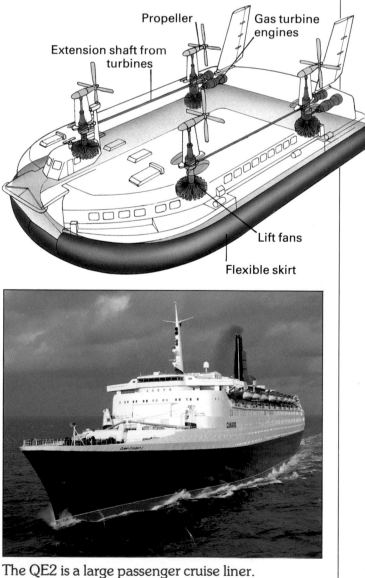

Propeller

Gas turbine engines

Extension shaft from turbines

Lift fans

Flexible skirt

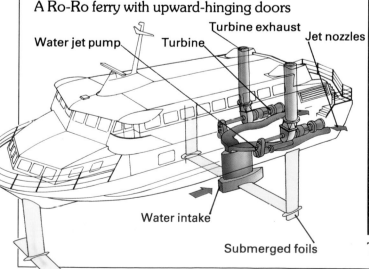

Water jet pump

Turbine

Turbine exhaust

Jet nozzles

Water intake

Submerged foils

The QE2 is a large passenger cruise liner.

Leisure craft

Sailing is a very popular leisure activity, with the boats used ranging from windsurfers to large yachts with cabin accommodation. The fastest designs are catamarans and trimarans, which carry large areas of sail but have only a small amount of hull moving through the water.

High-speed motorboats plane on the surface of the water instead of floating on it. They generally use outboard motors which combine the motor, drive and propeller in a single unit.

A cabin cruiser is a large motorboat.

A sailing boat powered only by the wind

Special-purpose ships

Exploration vessels, cruising the world's oceans, use sonar and seismic instruments to map the sea bed and its underlying rock structure. Techniques like this are used to find possible oil fields. Icebreakers have very strong hulls to withstand the crushing forces and shocks. The Soviet icebreaker *Sibir* has a 75,000 hp nuclear power plant and can operate in ice more than 4 m (13 ft) thick. Heavy loads such as drilling rigs can be moved using a semi-submersible heavy lift ship. The hull is submerged so that the load can be floated in place over the deck, then the lift ship resurfaces to support the load for transport.

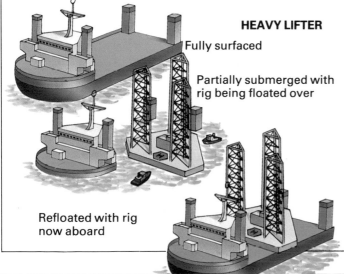

HEAVY LIFTER
Fully surfaced

Partially submerged with rig being floated over

Refloated with rig now aboard

An icebreaker pushing through pack ice

WARSHIPS AND SUBMARINES

The American aircraft carrier USS *Enterprise* is 335 m (1,102 ft) long and has eight nuclear reactors driving its turbines.

A nuclear-powered submarine can carry more than 16 guided missiles, each with up to 10 warheads.

Warships are floating carriers of weapons, from guns and torpedoes to missiles and even strike aircraft. A country uses its navy to defend itself and its overseas territories from sea-borne aggressors. It also uses naval vessels if necessary to protect cargo ships on trade routes. A country's navy can also be a formidable means of offense, employed to attack the ships and lands of its enemies. Aircraft carriers act as a base for warplanes; small warships are fast and maneuverable; naval submarines are invisible when submerged yet have enormous destructive power.

Warships

Warships range in size from huge aircraft carriers, which act as floating airfields for up to 100 attack aircraft, to tiny landing craft for ferrying invading troops ashore. The landing craft are carried on assault ships, which also have helicopters for reconnaissance and submarine detection. Carriers are supported by missile cruisers, and both types are protected by several destroyers and frigates, which deal with any enemy submarines. Support vessels keep the warships supplied with food, fuel and ammunition such as shells, torpedoes, missiles and bombs (for aircraft). Attack submarines patrol well away from the main fleet and are prepared to attack enemy vessels.

Shown right is a typical formation for a battle fleet.

Key

1 Aircraft carrier
2 Missile cruiser
3 Destroyer
4 Frigate
5 Assault ship
6 Landing craft
7 Support vessel
8 Attack submarine

Aircraft carrier and its planes

Destroyer refueling at sea

Submarines

Missile-carrying submarines have a massive destructive capability, with intercontinental missiles carrying multiple independently-controlled nuclear warheads over ranges of 8,000 km (5,000 miles) or more. Hunter-killer submarines are designed to track and destroy these missile carriers and also surface ships.

Many modern submarines are nuclear powered, and to avoid detection can remain submerged for months. Their hulls are covered with rubber tiles that absorb sound to confuse enemy sonar.

On the surface a submarine is kept afloat by the air in its ballast tanks (1). To dive, water is pumped into the tanks, displacing air (2) and reducing buoyancy (3). To surface, compressed air is released into the tanks (4), pushing the water out. When submerged a submarine can maneuver up and down using hydroplanes and turn with its rudder.

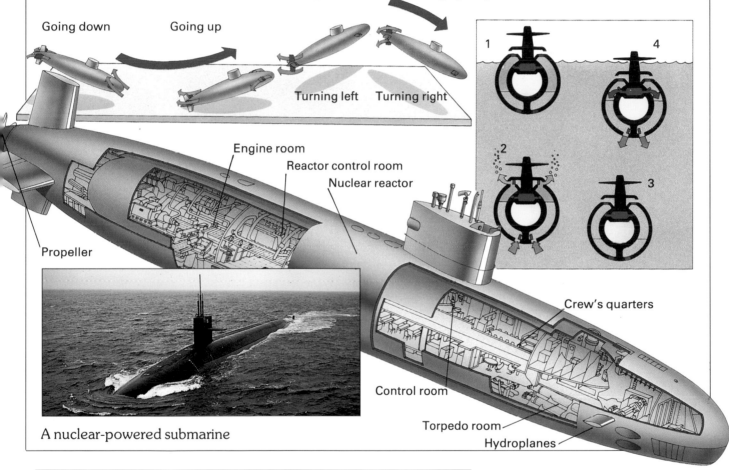

Going down   Going up

Turning left   Turning right

Engine room
Reactor control room
Nuclear reactor

Propeller

Crew's quarters

Control room

Torpedo room
Hydroplanes

A nuclear-powered submarine

Submersibles

Submersibles are small non-military submarines used for working on underwater structures like oil rigs and pipelines. They are also used for exploration and in deep salvage operations. Some submersibles carry operators who manipulate mechanical arms and tools mounted on the outside; others are remote-controlled from a mother ship at the surface. The manned submersible *Alvin* was used to explore the wreck of the *Titanic* 3,800 m (12,460 ft) below the waves of the North Atlantic.

A submersible research vessel

The first road vehicle with an internal combustion engine was made by Samuel Brown in 1826 and ran on coal gas.

Total production of the Volkswagen "Beetle" car exceeds 21 million.

Italy had over 80 vehicles per km (128 per mile) of road in 1985; the figure for the United States was 27 per km (43 per mile).

Cars and trucks are the most versatile forms of transport because they can carry people and a variety of goods over different kinds of journeys. Self-contained and compact drive systems give motor vehicles almost complete freedom of movement. The basic design can be adapted to meet most needs, from heavy haulage of outsize loads to off-road trucks and high-speed racing cars. But most traffic travels along roads, and there are strict regulations about how roads are built and used to ensure safe and reliable operation with the least possible conflict between different types of road user. Indeed the versatility and reliability of modern road transport has increased demand to such high levels that often traffic congestion prevents efficient operation.

Loads and conditions

Trucks can carry all sorts of loads directly to the place that they are required. To carry even more, some trucks tow trailers. In places with long straight roads, such as southern Australia, several trailers are towed to form long "road trains." Some countries have safety regulations to limit the maximum load that can be carried by a truck. In Europe and the United States, limits range from 38 to 50 tons, but other countries do not set limits.

Strict safety regulations are generally applied to buses. Where transport is less frequent, particularly in developing countries, all available space is occupied by passengers.

A typically overcrowded bus in India

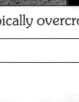

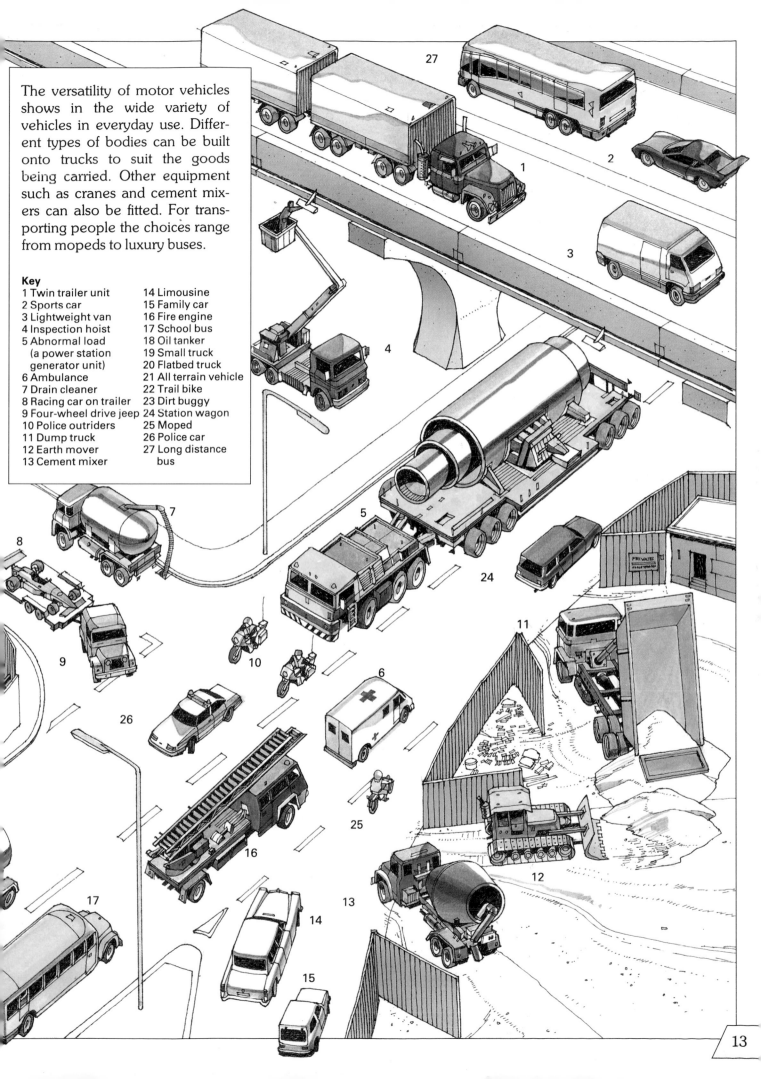

The versatility of motor vehicles shows in the wide variety of vehicles in everyday use. Different types of bodies can be built onto trucks to suit the goods being carried. Other equipment such as cranes and cement mixers can also be fitted. For transporting people the choices range from mopeds to luxury buses.

Key

1 Twin trailer unit
2 Sports car
3 Lightweight van
4 Inspection hoist
5 Abnormal load (a power station generator unit)
6 Ambulance
7 Drain cleaner
8 Racing car on trailer
9 Four-wheel drive jeep
10 Police outriders
11 Dump truck
12 Earth mover
13 Cement mixer
14 Limousine
15 Family car
16 Fire engine
17 School bus
18 Oil tanker
19 Small truck
20 Flatbed truck
21 All terrain vehicle
22 Trail bike
23 Dirt buggy
24 Station wagon
25 Moped
26 Police car
27 Long distance bus

BICYCLES AND MOTORCYCLES

The first bicycles did not have pedals; riders pushed them along using their feet.

Aerodynamic racing bicycles can reach speeds of more than 100 km/h (63 mph).

Japan makes more motor-cycles than any other country.

Bicycles are a convenient form of transport for short journeys, and the main means of personal transport in countries such as China. They are cheap to run, they do not create pollution and they take up only a little road space. Apart from poor weather protection, the main drawback of a bicycle is the vulnerability of the rider to other kinds of traffic. Many countries have special lanes to minimize this risk. Motorcycles started off as bicycles fitted with engines, and mopeds are still like this. But most modern motorcycles are more elaborate, with powerful engines and special tires and brakes.

Bicycles

On most bicycles the pedals drive the rear wheel through a chain. Gears make it easier to climb hills or go faster on the level. With the derailleur gear change, the chain is moved sideways to engage separate gear wheels of different diameters. In a low gear, pedal movement turns the wheel more slowly but with greater force than in a high gear.

Tandem bicycles have two or more seats and linked sets of pedals. Tricycles have three wheels and are easier for the rider to balance. Rickshaws are also three-wheeled and have passenger seats behind the rider. Similar machines with platforms instead of seats are used for carrying loads.

A bicycle parking space in a Chinese street

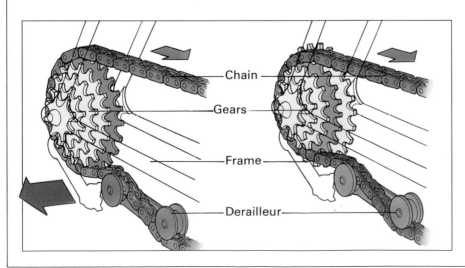

Chain

Gears

Frame

Derailleur

A rickshaw and driver

Motorcycles

Many types of motorcycle have been developed to meet different needs. Mopeds are cheap to run and easy to ride. They have small engines – under 50 cc – that give a top speed of around 50 km/h (30 mph). Scooters also have small engines, and provide more protection for the rider's legs.

Cruise bikes are large, powerful machines suitable for riding over long distances. Padded seats, fairings and windscreens ensure comfort, and there are big luggage containers. Rugged construction is a feature of motorcycles for off-road use or trials racing. Knobbly tires give good grip and the telescopic suspension soaks up bumps.

A motorcyclist with a young passenger

A trials bike crosses rough ground

A cruise bike for long-distance comfort

The modern motorcycle

A typical modern motorcycle has a gasoline engine driving the rear wheel through a gearbox and chain or shaft. Engines may be two- or four-stroke and air- or water-cooled.

A small 125 cc motorbike weighs around 100 kg (220 lb) and the 12 hp engine gives a top speed of around 110 km/h (70 mph). Bigger engines of around 1,000 cc can produce 100 hp or more. Machines in this class accelerate faster than most cars and readily reach 200 km/h (125 mph). Disk brakes and tough tires are generally fitted to ensure the stopping power matches the performance.

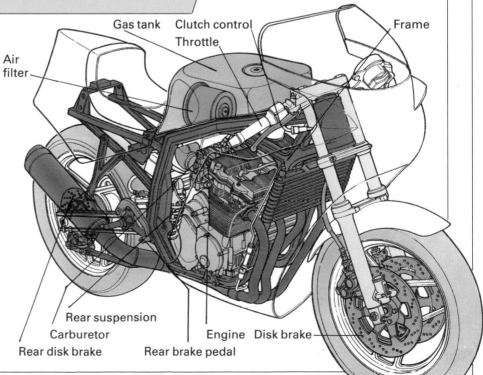

Gas tank   Clutch control   Frame
Throttle
Air filter
Rear suspension
Carburetor
Rear disk brake   Rear brake pedal   Engine   Disk brake

CARS

The first gasoline-driven car was built by Karl Benz in Germany in 1885. Its top speed was 16 km/h (10 mph).

Many cars have top speeds of more than 160 km/h (100 mph), but most countries have speed limits that are lower than this.

The invention and mass production of the motor car revolutionized personal transport. Continued development in the hundred years since the first car has produced comfortable and reliable vehicles that give people the freedom to travel where they want when they want, so long as there is a road or track. This freedom shows most strongly in the United States, where there were 724 cars per 1,000 population by 1985, traveling a total of nearly 7 billion passenger kilometers (4.35 billion miles) a year. But in cities, the large number of cars has caused traffic congestion.

Car layout

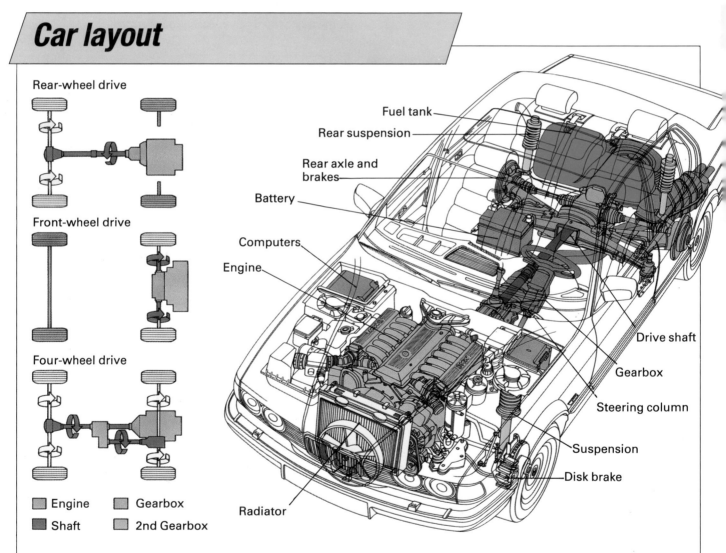

Rear-wheel drive

Front-wheel drive

Four-wheel drive

- ◻ Engine
- ◼ Shaft
- ◻ Gearbox
- ◻ 2nd Gearbox

Fuel tank
Rear suspension
Rear axle and brakes
Battery
Computers
Engine
Radiator
Drive shaft
Gearbox
Steering column
Suspension
Disk brake

In a rear-wheel drive car, power from the engine passes through the clutch and gearbox. Starting from rest needs high torque so a low gear is selected; as the speed increases higher gears are engaged. From the gearbox a drive (or propeller) shaft runs to the differential. This lets the driven wheels run at different speeds around corners.

In front-wheel drive the engine, gearbox and differential form an integrated power unit with short drive shafts to the wheels. Four-wheel drive is mechanically more complex, generally requiring two gearboxes, but gives safe and consistent handling and good traction on poor or slippery surfaces.

Car types

Cars come in a wide variety of types to suit different needs. These range from the roomy station wagon, with a large luggage capacity, to high performance sports cars with just enough room for the driver and a passenger, and from prestige limousines to family sedans. The development of a new model is highly complicated and takes several years. As a result new models appear in several versions, which share the same engine and drive layout.

A car in a wind tunnel

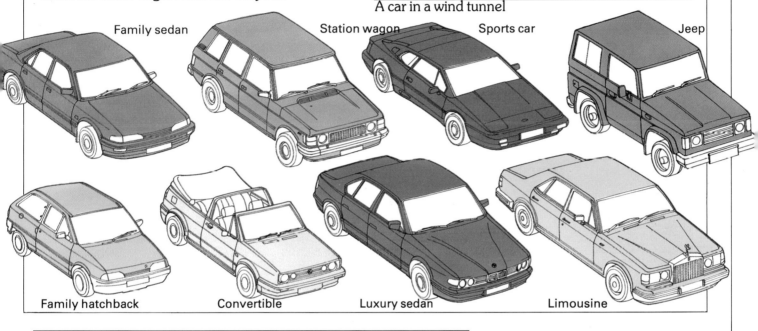

Family sedan   Station wagon   Sports car   Jeep

Family hatchback   Convertible   Luxury sedan   Limousine

Safety

A lot of effort goes into making sure that modern car designs are safe. Good roadholding and features such as anti-lock brakes give primary safety by making it less likely that the car will be involved in an accident. But if an accident does occur modern cars have secondary safety features that reduce the chances that occupants will be injured.

A car's front and back body sections crumple on impact to absorb the shock, and dangerous surfaces – such as the instrument panel and steering wheel – are padded. Seat belts stop the car occupants from being thrown around inside the car.

Crash tests are carried out to check the strength of construction and to study the effects of collisions on passengers. The car is fitted with impact-measuring sensors and instrumented dummies are placed in the front seats. The car is then propelled at 48 km/h (30 mph) into a concrete block.

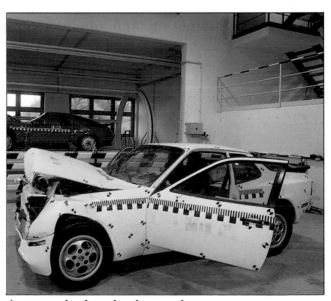
A car crashed to check on safety

Computers in the modern car

Computers and microprocessors are finding increasing use in modern cars, monitoring and controlling the operation of many different systems. Engine management systems use sensors to measure such things as how hard the engine is working, speed and exhaust emission. The system continuously adjusts the ignition timing and air-fuel mixture to give peak performance and economy. Power steering is also regulated in relation to the car's speed.

Active suspension systems use an electronic control unit with sensors and hydraulic pistons to adjust the individual suspension units in response to bumps, giving a smooth and level ride.

Anti-lock brake systems (ABS) continually check four to ten times a second to make sure the wheels have not stopped turning while braking. If they have, brake pressure is reduced to let the wheel start turning again. This can reduce braking distances by up to 40 per cent.

A modern car's main computer

Computer navigation system

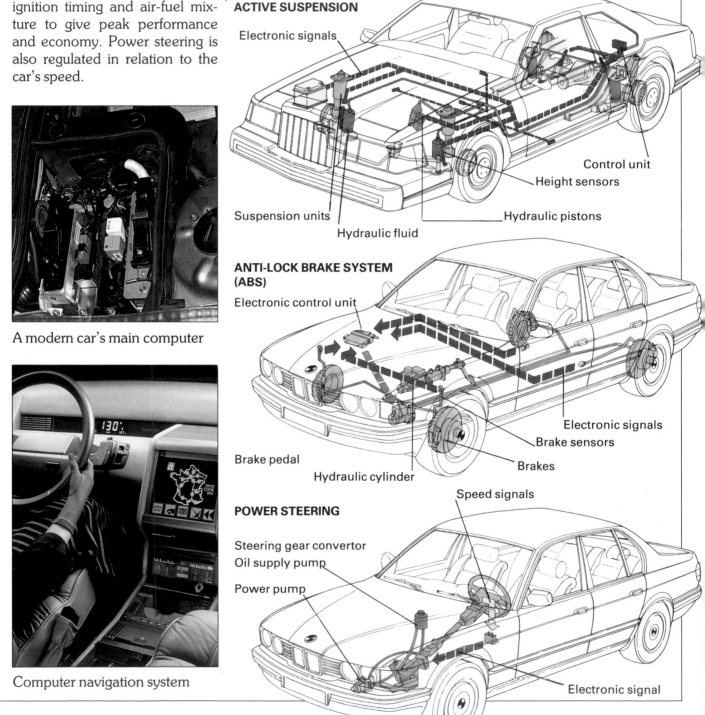

ACTIVE SUSPENSION

Electronic signals

Control unit

Height sensors

Hydraulic pistons

Suspension units

Hydraulic fluid

ANTI-LOCK BRAKE SYSTEM (ABS)

Electronic control unit

Electronic signals

Brake sensors

Brake pedal

Brakes

Hydraulic cylinder

Speed signals

POWER STEERING

Steering gear convertor

Oil supply pump

Power pump

Electronic signal

Racing cars

High speed and good roadholding are the essential features of racing cars. Most spectacular are the Formula One single-seaters. Wide, smooth tires give a good grip, the back ones being bigger to transmit the engine power. Downthrust from the aerodynamically designed body forces it down onto the road so that the tires can generate more cornering power. The 3.5-liter engines used for the 1989 season produce more than 600 hp; earlier 1.5-liter turbocharged engines had peak outputs of over 1,000 hp.

Sports car racers and rally cars look more like road vehicles, but can be very different under the surface. Bodies are often made from lightweight, high-strength materials such as carbon fiber, and the engine and transmission systems are highly modified. New ideas tried out in these cars can find their way into normal road cars – the modern trend to four-wheel drive was stimulated by the Audi Quattro rally car of the early 1980s.

An unusual six-wheeled racing car

Coaches and buses

Coaches are an important means of public transport and can cover long distance at high speeds. Some services, like those across North America and Australia, take several days to complete their journeys. For passenger comfort, modern coaches are often air conditioned, have a bathroom and may have video entertainment systems.

Buses are used for shorter trips, generally in towns and urban areas. They run on regular routes with frequent stops. They often transport many working commuters, and separate bus lanes help reduce delays caused by traffic congestion. A typical design such as the MAN SL220 is 12.2 m (40 ft) long, has a 207 hp engine and can carry 60 passengers, some standing. Greater capacity is provided by articulated designs and double-deckers.

A luxury coach for high-speed road travel

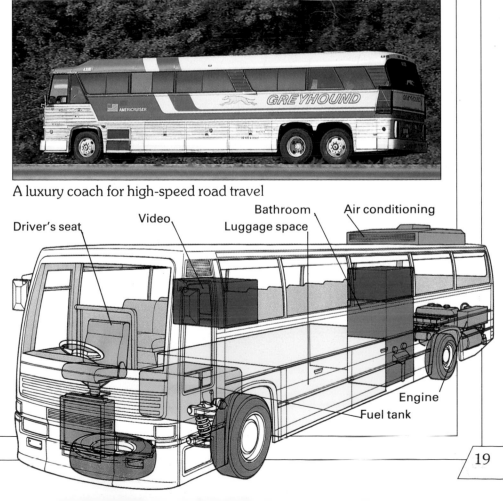

Driver's seat · Video · Bathroom · Air conditioning · Luggage space · Engine · Fuel tank

The heaviest loads regularly carried by road are parts of oil drilling rigs which can weigh as much as 3,800 tons.

Off-road dump trucks can carry loads of over 300 tons.

Big trucks are often called juggernauts (an Indian word).

Trucks are designed for constant hard use with maximum reliability. They generally use diesel engines, which are economical and very sturdy, although they do add to atmospheric pollution. In most trucks the engine is fitted at the front of the cab, which can be tilted up to give access.

Trucks for heavy loads have several axles to spread the weight, and the extra rear axles are usually driven to give better traction. Additional loads can be carried in trailers. In Australia trucks of up to 400 hp pull two or three trailers at a time. This is known as a road train.

Articulated trucks

Big trucks are often articulated – they have a tractor unit which provides the power while the load is carried in a semi-trailer. The trailer has wheels at the rear and is supported by the tractor unit at the front, the two parts being connected by a special coupling known as a fifth wheel. This arrangement makes it easy to disconnect the tractor and attach another trailer.

The fifth wheel also lets the trailer pivot, making the complete vehicle easier to maneuver. However, under certain conditions jack-knifing can occur, with the trailer overrunning the tractor so that the coupling is forced into a sharp angle.

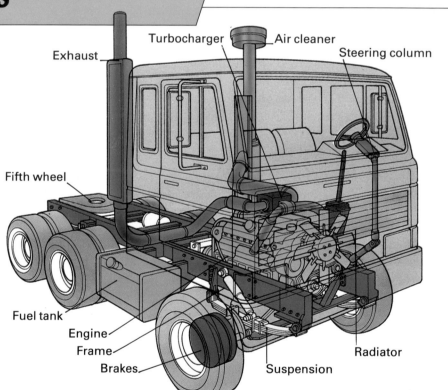

Exhaust · Turbocharger · Air cleaner · Steering column · Fifth wheel · Fuel tank · Engine · Frame · Brakes · Suspension · Radiator

Powerful road trains cross the Australian desert.

Off road

To give them grip and to stop them sinking into soft ground, off-road vehicles have four-wheel drive and very big tires, or run on caterpillar tracks. The tracks consist of a series of flat plates hinged together to form a continuous loop. Toothed drive wheels carry the track forward, laying it down to give a solid path for the load-carrying wheels.

Runners are used for vehicles that run on snow. Some designs have tracks or a wide rubber belt for the drive, and are steered by turning the front runners.

Amphibious vehicles have a watertight boat-like body that will float in water. This lets them drive off land into the water, travel along under power, and drive back onto land. Some have propellers driven by the engine; with others the road wheels and tires act as paddle wheels to push the vehicle along in the water.

An earth-moving vehicle has huge tires.

Caterpillar tracks work well on snow.

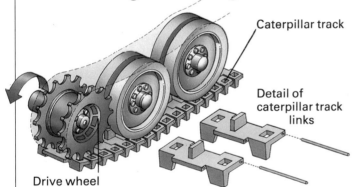
Caterpillar track

Detail of caterpillar track links

Drive wheel

An amphibious vehicle takes to the water.

Heavy loads

Heavy loads are moved on the roads using special trailers pulled by road tractors. The Faun heavy road tractor has engine outputs of up to 986 hp and can pull loads of up to 300 tons. Three or four tractors coupled together are used for bigger loads.

One very heavy load is the U.S. Space Shuttle, which is prepared in a large building nearly 6 km (3.7 miles) away from the launch pad. It is then carried to the launch pad standing upright on a huge tracked crawler. This crawler is the biggest land vehicle ever made and was first used to carry the Saturn 5 Moon rocket.

The world's biggest land transporter

French electric TGV services between Paris and Lyon average 212 km/h (132 mph). Top speed is 270 km/h (168 mph).

The first public steam railroad – the Stockton and Darlington – opened in 1825.

New York City's Grand Central Station has 67 platforms, all below ground.

The most powerful steam engine was the 1916 Mallett of the Virginia Railroad.

The self-guiding action of flanged wheels running on metal rails, combined with smooth tracks laid to gentle gradients, make railroad a good and economical way of moving large numbers of people and large quantities of goods. Advanced passenger services with trains running at speeds of over 260 km/h (165 mph) make short travel times between city centers. They are fast enough to compete with aircraft for distances up to 500 km (300 miles) or so. Within cities, passenger services are provided by underground trains, or by cable cars and trolley buses running in the streets. General freight traffic is consolidated into trains in marshaling yards. Bulk loads such as coal and mineral ores are hauled in fixed train sets with 100 or more wagons and a weight of 10,000 tons.

Steam locomotives

Steam power made railroads possible. In a steam locomotive the fuel, normally coal, is burned to heat water in a boiler. This makes steam which drives pistons to make the wheels go around. Operating a steam locomotive involves a lot of hard and dirty work with a crew of at least two, driver and fireman, being needed. Firing the boiler to generate steam, keeping the engine supplied with coal and water, disposing of the ash, and general servicing are all time-consuming and restrict the actual running time.

Steam locomotives still run in China.

A busy station has both high-speed intercity expresses and local commuter services. Passengers arriving at the station can transfer to subway trains, cable cars or trolley buses to travel around within the city.

Key
1 Diesel locomotive
2 Freight shunter
3 Steam locomotive (Mallard)
4 Diesel electric locomotive
5 High speed electric train (TGV)
6 Local commuter train
7 Electric subway train
8 Trolley bus
9 Cable car
10 Suspended monorail
11 Freight wagons
12 Double deck passenger coach

The biggest freight train was an American one that had six locomotives and 500 coal wagons. It stretched for 6 km (3 ¾ miles).

The longest rail route is 9,438 km (5,864 miles) on the Soviet Trans-Siberia line. It runs from Moscow to Nakhodka.

Modern railroads use diesel electric or electric traction. Diesel-electric locomotives have diesel engines that drive generators, whereas electric locomotives have electric motors powered by electricity picked up from overhead wires or electrified rails. Electric systems are preferred to diesel electric for busy lines where the high cost of installing the line is offset by lower running costs. Passenger trains which may only have two or three coaches have the motors or engines built into the coaches. Heavy trains particularly for freight have two or more locomotives with linked controls.

Freight locomotives

Diesel engines are a compact and reliable power source for locomotives and are produced with engines of up to 6,600 hp, although maximum ratings around 3,000 hp are more usual. In diesel-hydraulic locomotives the diesel engine powers a hydraulic pump to give high pressure oil. This is then used to work a hydraulic motor connected to the driving wheels. Diesel-electric drives are more common. The engines drive generators and the electricity produced powers electric traction motors.

Electric locomotives pick up power through contact shoes sliding on conductor rails, or by pantographs that extend up to overhead wires. Several different supply voltages are in use, ranging from 600 volts direct current (DC) to 25,000 volts alternating current (AC). This powers the motor directly.

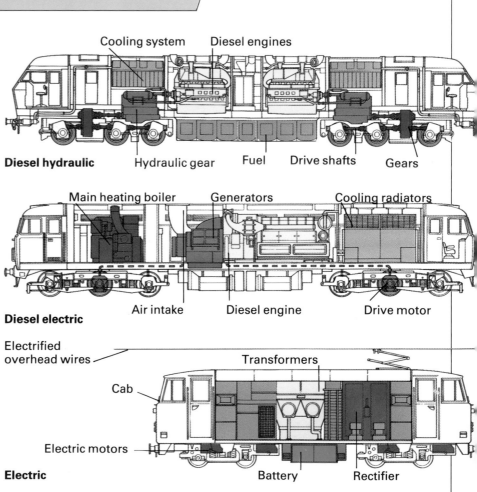

Diesel hydraulic
Cooling system   Diesel engines   Hydraulic gear   Fuel   Drive shafts   Gears

Diesel electric
Main heating boiler   Generators   Cooling radiators   Air intake   Diesel engine   Drive motor

Electric
Electrified overhead wires   Transformers   Cab   Electric motors   Battery   Rectifier

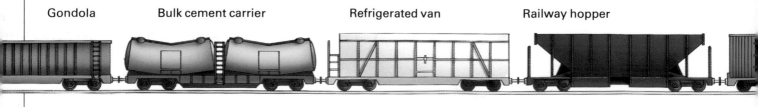

Gondola   Bulk cement carrier   Refrigerated van   Railway hopper

Passenger stock

Commuter coaches have to carry large numbers of passengers – who sometimes have to stand. As long as there is enough clearance under bridges and in tunnels double-decker carriages can be used. Canadian bi-level commuter cars in Toronto have seats for 162 passengers and a maximum crush capacity of 438. Long-distance trains are more luxurious, with greater passenger space and facilities such as dining cars and sleeping cars.

Sleeper bunks in a Chinese train

Electric trains on the French railroad

Freight

Flat freight cars allow easy transfer of cargo containers from trucks; alternatively, complete loaded trucks can be carried on low-loaders. Materials such as grain and cement are transported in covered hoppers designed for easy loading and unloading. Efficient freight operations rely on computers to keep track of the individual loads. The highly automated Mascher marshaling yard near Hamburg in West Germany can sort up to 700 wagons an hour.

A freight container being unloaded

Freight wagons in a marshaling yard

Containers on flat car   Coal hopper

Bulk grain hopper   Car transporter

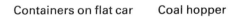

Numbers of passengers carried underground each year:
London – 650 million
New York – 990 million
Tokyo – 1.85 billion

Hong Kong's metro can take 75,000 passengers an hour in each direction.

Space in city centers is often very limited, and crowded roads make it difficult to operate buses and cable cars. One of the best solutions is to go underground because the only space needed on the surface is for entrances to the ticket halls. This was first done in London in 1863 and many cities now have extensive underground railroad systems.

Frequent peak-hour services provide a large carrying capacity, making underground systems one of the most effective ways of quickly moving people around in cities.

Tube trains

Large subway systems have several separate lines – 23 in New York, seven in Tokyo, nine in London – with passenger interchanges at the stations. A complicated network of tunnels is needed to let passengers move from the entrance and ticket halls down to the platforms, and between one line and another. Passengers use an escalator or stairs to get down to and back up from the tunnels. Rail tunnels are built on different levels so they can pass over or under each other.

Tunnels are dug well below the foundations of buildings – the deepest one in London is 67 m (221 ft) below the surface. Where possible shallower tunnels are run along under roads, while surface tracks are used away from the city center. Some systems also have elevated tracks; the New York Subway has 220 km (138 miles) underground and 150 km (94 miles) elevated.

Electric traction is always used, commonly with a 600-volt DC supply through a third rail. To slow down, the power to the motors is switched off and the motor helps act as a brake.

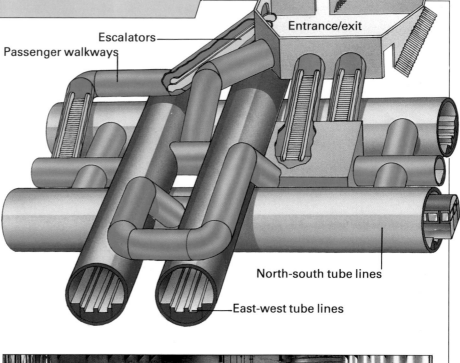

Escalators
Passenger walkways
Entrance/exit
North-south tube lines
East-west tube lines

Many cities have underground railroads.

Driverless trains

Most underground trains run on simple routes, which makes them particularly suitable for automatic control. Closed-circuit television lets supervisors in a control center keep a continuous watch on operations so they can rapidly intervene if anything goes wrong. The Lille Metro in France was specifically designed for driverless operation and carries over 120,000 passengers a day with trains every minute in peak periods. The platforms have doors that open only when they are lined up with the train doors.

A fully automated, driverless train

Channel Tunnel

The Channel Tunnel is being dug under the English Channel to connect England and France. It is due to start carrying traffic in 1993. The total length is 50 km (31 miles), 38 of them (24 miles) actually under the Channel.

Two main running tunnels have tracks to carry trains, with a smaller service tunnel running between them. Passenger and goods trains will run directly through the tunnel, linking the British and French railroad networks. Cars will be carried through on special shuttle trains running between terminals at each end of the tunnel. Cars and trucks will drive onto the shuttle wagons, and travel through the tunnel in about 35 minutes.

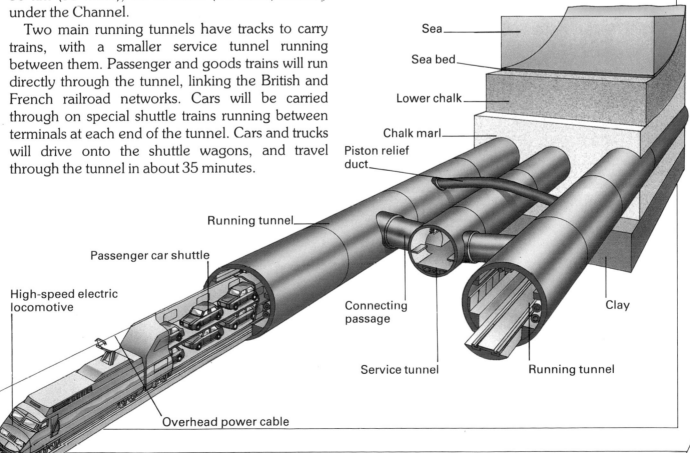

Sea

Sea bed

Lower chalk

Chalk marl

Piston relief duct

Running tunnel

Passenger car shuttle

High-speed electric locomotive

Connecting passage

Clay

Service tunnel

Running tunnel

Overhead power cable

The Mount Pilatus rack railroad in Switzerland has a 1 in 2 gradient.

Electric cable cars were first used in Blackpool, U.K. in 1884.

Mine railroads, with man-pushed trucks running on rails, were in use before 1550.

Cable cars and trolley buses are electric vehicles that pick up current from overhead wires. Cable cars run on rails, like a train, whereas a trolley bus can be steered like a bus. Both are particularly suitable for use in cities because they can make use of the existing road network. They are gradually coming back into more general use. Monorail systems are also good for cities because the track can be readily run over roads and rivers. Cableways are used for both goods and passenger transport, where it is impossible to lay conventional tracks.

Monorail

Monorail systems have only one rail and the train is either hung from it or balanced over it, as the various systems (right) show. The Wuppertal monorail system in Germany is a suspended design that has been operating since 1901 and carries around 16 million passengers a year. There are 19 stations on the 13.3 km (8.3 mile) track, a lot of it running over the Wupper River.

With the other type of monorail the coaches straddle the track, which can be made from steel or cast concrete. Support wheels run on top of the track and separate stabilizing wheels bear on the track sides. The monorail from Tokyo to Haneda airport in Japan uses this arrangement, with trains making the 13-km (8-mile) run in 15 minutes. Hovertrains are a development of this principle. They work by using a low-friction air cushion for support.

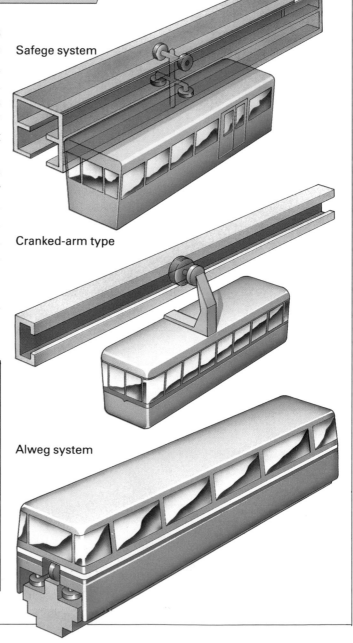

Safege system

Cranked-arm type

Alweg system

A monorail train using the Alweg system

Cable cars and trolley buses

Both cable cars and trolley buses run along existing roads. Most use electric motors, usually collecting power from overhead wires. The main difference between them is that cable cars run on rails set in the road surface whereas trolley buses have tires and are steered like buses.

Cable cars and trolley bus services used to operate in a lot of cities, but most of them were slow and uncomfortable and they were gradually replaced by motor buses. Modern designs are reversing the trend, offering fast, comfortable and pollution-free urban transport. For example, the new French standard cable car has an articulated twin carriage 94ft long and 8ft wide. It can carry 168 passengers, 108 of them standing, and has a maximum speed of 80 km/h (50 mph).

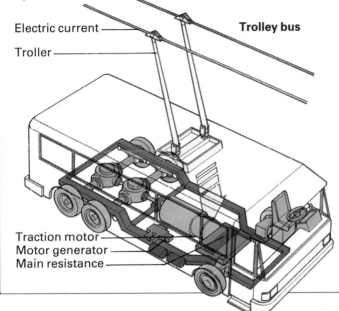

Electric current

Troller

Trolley bus

Traction motor
Motor generator
Main resistance

An articulated cable car

Mines and industry

Special railroads are used to carry materials in mines and factories. They often have narrow tracks, and some systems are automatically controlled. Cableways are used for coal and metal ores. The cables run between a series of support towers and carry load buckets that are automatically emptied at one end. Long runs are possible: one Swedish cableway is 96 km (60 miles) long and carries 50 tons an hour.

A narrow-gauge mineral railroad

Maglev

Maglev, or magnetic levitation, systems have powerful magnets in the track and in the train. These repel one another so that the carriages float just above the track. A linear electric motor stretched along the track is used for propulsion. The smooth ride and very low friction make high speeds possible – an experimental Japanese maglev system has carried passengers at more than 400 km/h (250 mph).

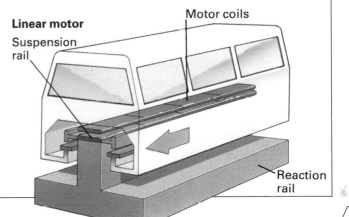

Linear motor

Motor coils

Suspension rail

Reaction rail

The solar power car *Sunracer* travelled 3,138 km (1,950 miles) across Australia in a time of two-and-a-half days.

Marine diesel engines have cylinders up to 1 m (3.25 ft) in diameter.

Electric motors are compact and clean power sources, but the electricity has to be generated somewhere else and fed to the motor. With electric trains this can be done using rails or overhead wires, but this method is not suitable for other kinds of electric transport and batteries have to be used.

Most ships use large diesel engines which are efficient and use readily available fuel. Gas turbines are compact and lightweight, but have high fuel consumptions. They are used where very high power is required – as in some warships. Nuclear power is also used in some vessels.

Electric motors (right) have two parts carrying wire coils: the rotor, which can turn, and the stator, which is fixed. Current flowing through the coils produces magnetic fields that push against one another so that the rotor turns. Electric motors can be driven by either direct or alternating current and have control systems for smooth starting and speed control.

In steam locomotives, valves (below) are used to admit steam to each side of a piston in turn, driving it back and forth. A connecting rod transfers piston movement to the wheels, making them turn. Advanced steam locomotive designs (below right) use special systems to burn coal efficiently, and have circuits to condense the steam and return it to the boiler, so minimizing water consumption.

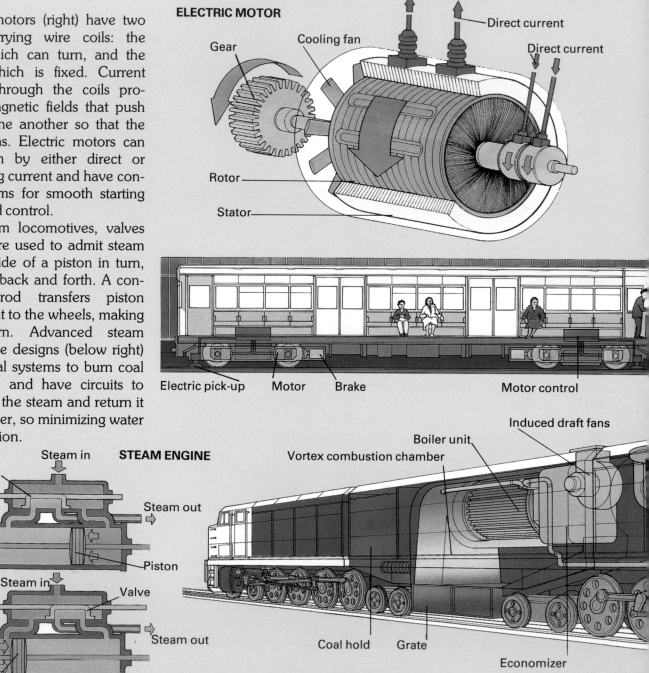

ELECTRIC MOTOR

Gear

Cooling fan

Direct current

Direct current

Rotor

Stator

Electric pick-up   Motor   Brake   Motor control

STEAM ENGINE

Steam in

Valve

Steam out

Piston

Steam in

Valve

Steam out

Piston

Induced draft fans

Boiler unit

Vortex combustion chamber

Coal hold   Grate

Economizer

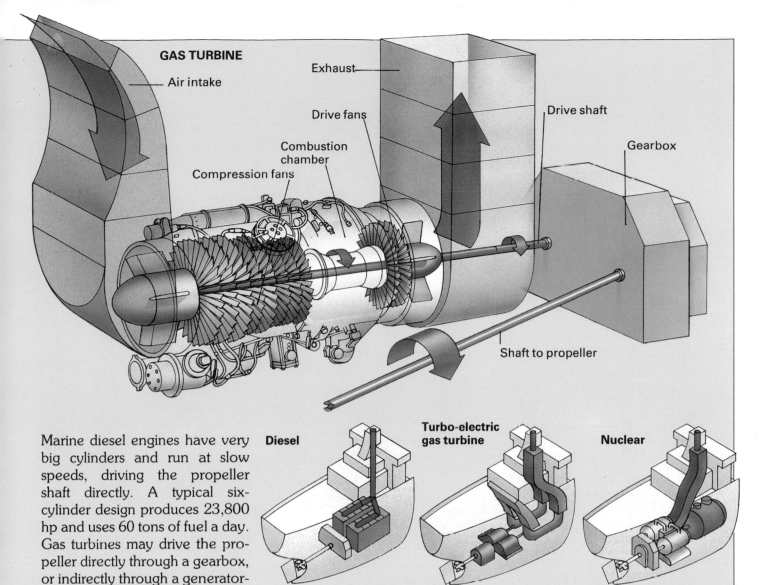

GAS TURBINE

Air intake

Exhaust

Drive fans

Drive shaft

Combustion chamber

Gearbox

Compression fans

Shaft to propeller

Marine diesel engines have very big cylinders and run at slow speeds, driving the propeller shaft directly. A typical six-cylinder design produces 23,800 hp and uses 60 tons of fuel a day. Gas turbines may drive the propeller directly through a gearbox, or indirectly through a generator-motor arrangement which allows flexible control. In nuclear ships the reactor is used to produce superheated steam that drives a steam turbine.

Diesel

Turbo-electric gas turbine

Nuclear

Sails are being used to assist the engines in some experimental ships. The sails are rigid and automatically set to match the wind direction by a computer control system. A fuel saving of 10 to 20 per cent is obtained without any loss of performance.

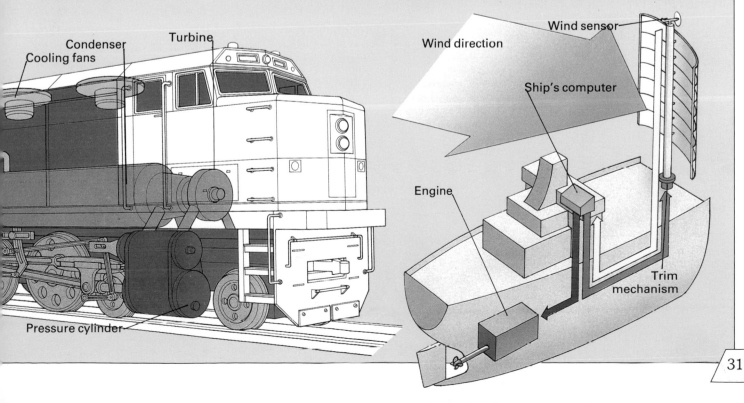

Cooling fans

Condenser

Turbine

Wind sensor

Wind direction

Ship's computer

Engine

Pressure cylinder

Trim mechanism

Internal combustion engines produce power by exploding a fuel/air mixture in a cylinder. This drives a piston up and down, and the movement turns the engine crankshaft through a connecting rod.

Most cars, and a lot of other vehicles, use gasoline or spark ignition engines. Air is sucked into the engine cylinders through a carburetor, which mixes in the gasoline at a ratio of approximately 15 parts air to 1 part gasoline by weight. The mixture is compressed to about one-tenth of its volume and is ignited by an electric spark at the spark plug. The spark is produced by the ignition system and is supplied to each cylinder at the right time by the distributor.

Engine sizes are stated in terms of the volume swept out by the piston movement, and a typical car engine produces around 55 hp. Tuned engines for racing cars have outputs of up to 200 hp per liter, while more power is obtained by using turbochargers.

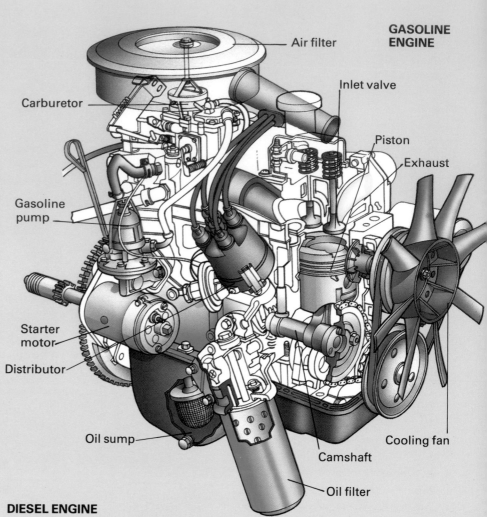

GASOLINE ENGINE

Air filter
Inlet valve
Piston
Exhaust
Carburetor
Gasoline pump
Starter motor
Distributor
Oil sump
Cooling fan
Camshaft
Oil filter

DIESEL ENGINE

Diesel engines have compression ratios up to 20:1 and compression of the air in the cylinder raises its temperature to around 600°C (1,112°F). Liquid fuel is sprayed directly into the cylinder through an injector nozzle, and the high temperature makes it burn immediately.

Because of the high compression pressures, diesel engines have to be more solidly built and heavier than gasoline engines of the same capacity. Power output is often lower as well. However diesel engines are more economical and have an efficiency of up to 40 per cent compared to 30 per cent for spark ignition engines.

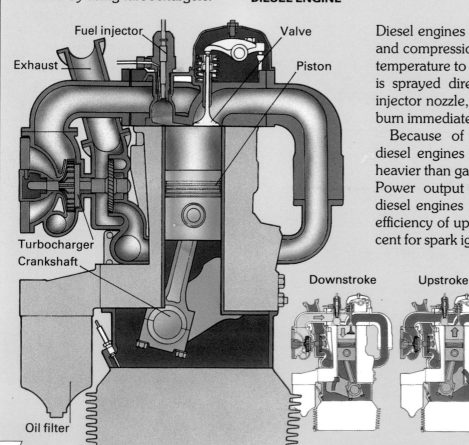

Fuel injector
Valve
Exhaust
Piston
Turbocharger
Crankshaft
Oil filter

Downstroke   Upstroke   Downstroke   Upstroke

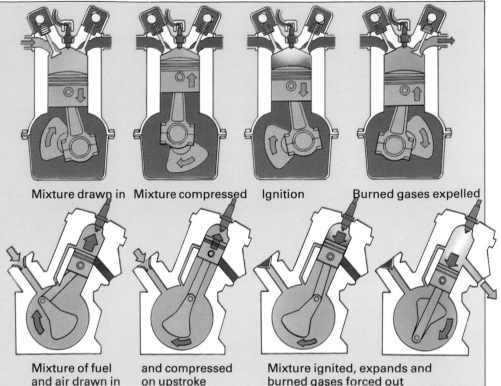

Four-stroke cycle: first down-stroke sucks fuel/air mixture into the cylinder; upstroke compresses the mixture, which is ignited by a spark; burning mixture expands to force the piston down; upstroke pushes the used mixture out of the exhaust, emptying the cylinder ready for the next cycle.

Mixture drawn in Mixture compressed Ignition Burned gases expelled

Two-stroke cycle: upstroke compresses the mixture in the cylinder and sucks mixture into the sealed crankcase underneath the piston; ignition and burning forces the piston down; at the end of the stroke burned mixture escapes through the exhaust and fresh mixture is forced into the cylinder from the crankcase.

Mixture of fuel and air drawn in

and compressed on upstroke

Mixture ignited, expands and burned gases forced out

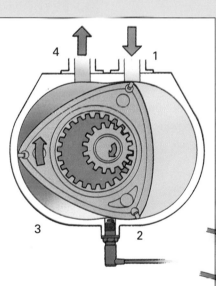

In the Wankel engine the piston is replaced by a triangular rotor. The rotor turns and rocks in a figure-eight shaped housing to give a series of chambers that expand and contract to carry out the normal four-stroke operating cycle. There are seals on the tips and sides of the rotor to separate the working chambers. As the rotor moves, an internal gear drives the central output shaft.

With fuel-injection systems, gasoline is injected into the engine inlet manifold as a fine spray that quickly mixes with the air. A control system adjusts the spray to give the correct proportions of gasoline and air.

FUEL INJECTION

Fuel injector

Inlet valve

Spark plug

Exhaust gases out

Compressed air goes to piston

Air drawn in

Turbine

TURBOCHARGER

Exhaust gases in

Engine power depends on the amount of fuel/air mixture burned in each cycle. Normally this is limited by the way the mixture has to be sucked into the cylinder, but higher power can be obtained by pushing extra air and fuel in with a turbocharger. Hot exhaust gases from the cylinders rapidly rotate a turbine to drive a centrifugal compressor. The compressed air is then fed to the engine cylinders.

Land speed records are of two types: where the vehicle is driven through its wheels, and where it is powered by rocket or jet thrust. Driving through the wheels means the tires have to take all the engine power as well as supporting the vehicle. This limits the maximum speed that can be achieved. Very flat surfaces are needed for record attempts because even the smallest bump would throw the car up into the air.

Similarly, boats can be jet-propelled or driven by propellers. Pushing a boat through the water at high speeds takes a lot more power than moving on wheels. The greater resistance to motion means that water speed records are slower than those on land. Smooth flat rails use even less power and automatically guide the vehicle. Because of this the very fastest land speeds are achieved by rocket-powered test sleds running on rails. However, they do not carry passengers.

High-speed boats and land vehicles have to have smooth bodies so that the air flows over them smoothly. A poor shape causes a lot of drag, which uses up the engine power. It may also make the vehicle or boat unstable so that the driver loses control. Many record breakers have been killed because they lost control at high speed.

WATER RECORDS

World water speed record: Kenneth Peter Warby, *Spirit of Australia*, 1978. 511.11 km/h (317.6 mph).

Fastest propeller-driven boat: Eddie Hill, *The Texan*, 1982. 368.5 km/h (229 mph).

Fastest Atlantic Crossing: Richard Branson, *Virgin Atlantic Challenger II*, 1986. 3 days 8 hours 31 minutes.

Fastest Atlantic crossing under sail: Serge Madec, *Jet Services 5 Catamaran*, 1988. 7 days 6 hours 30 minutes.

Fastest Channel crossing: SRN4 hovercraft, 24 minutes.

Virgin Atlantic Challenger II

LAND RECORDS

World land speed record (jet-powered): Richard Noble, *Thrust 2*, 1983. 1019.4 km/h (633.4 mph).

Fastest wheel-driven car: Donald Campbell, *Bluebird*, 1964. 690.9 km/h (429.3 mph).

Fastest steam car: Robert Barber, *Steaming Demon*, 1985. 234 km/h (145.6 mph).

Fastest diesel car: Mercedes, 1978. 327.3 km/h (203.3 mph).

Fastest human-powered vehicle: John Seibert, 1980. 99.7 km/h (61.9 mph).

The jet-powered car *Thrust 2*

RAIL RECORDS

Fastest steam locomotive: British *Mallard*, 1938. 202.8 km/h (126 mph).

Highest speed on rails (unmanned): US rocket test sled, 1982. 9,851 km/h (6,121 mph).

Fastest passenger transport: West German experimental train, 1988. 403 km/h (252 mph).

Fastest diesel train: British Rail High-Speed Train, 1973. 232 km/h (143 mph).

Fastest electric train: French Railways TGV, 1981. 380 km/h (236 mph).

The steam locomotive *Mallard*

acceleration the rate at which speed increases. The higher the acceleration, the faster a vehicle reaches a set speed.

aerodynamics study of the way objects move through the air.

amphibious describing a vehicle that can travel on both land and water.

articulated describing a truck with two sections connected by a flexible joint.

automatic gearbox gearbox with a control system that selects the right gear for the vehicle speed and load.

bathyscape deep-sea diving machine with a very strong ball-shaped cabin suspended from a large float.

carburetor device that mixes gasoline and air in the correct proportions for an internal combustion engine.

catamaran boat with twin hulls connected by a deck above the water.

clipper fast sailing ship once used for high-value cargos such as tea.

conductor wire or bar carrying an electric current.

crankshaft main shaft of an engine with offset cranks. Used to convert up and down movements into rotary motion.

diesel engine internal combustion engine in which the fuel is ignited by heat which is produced as air is compressed in the engine cylinders.

drag resistance to motion caused by a fluid, such as water or air, flowing past a moving body.

engine management system computer system that continually checks the performance of an engine and adjusts the control settings for peak performance.

four-stroke cycle engine cycle that takes four strokes of a piston, or two crankshaft revolutions, to complete.

gasoline engine internal combustion engine that uses gasoline as the fuel. The fuel/air mixture is ignited by a spark.

generator machine for converting mechanical energy into electrical energy.

internal combustion engine engine in which the fuel is burned inside the working cylinders, for example gasoline and diesel engines. Steam engines use external combustion.

linear electric motor electric motor in which the rotor and stator have been unrolled into flat sections to give straight-line movement.

maglev system using magnets to make vehicles float above a track.

microprocessor complete computer processing unit formed on a single silicon chip.

nuclear reactor enclosed assembly of radioactive material that can sustain nuclear fission. Heat is produced and can be used to boil water into steam for driving turbines.

outrigger float extended to one side of narrow-hulled boat to increase stability.

radar method of finding the direction and distance of objects, including aircraft and ships, by bouncing radio waves off them.

Ro-Ro ferries ferries with ramps that allow vehicles to drive on and off.

rudder hinged flap used for steering ships and boats.

skirt flexible seal fitted around the edge of a hovercraft to hold the air cushion in.

snorkel tube used to supply air to a submarine submerged just below the surface.

solar cell device for converting sunlight into electrical energy.

sonar method of detecting underwater objects, such as submarines, by sending out high-frequency sound pulses and listening for echoes.

steam turbine turbine that uses steam as the working fluid.

transformer device for altering the voltage of an alternating current electricity supply.

transmission system of gears and drive shafts that carries power from an engine to the driven wheels of a vehicle.

trimaran boat with three hulls joined together by a deck above sea level.

turbocharger air compressor used to force extra air into the cylinders of an internal combustion engine.

two-stroke cycle engine cycle in which the complete working cycle takes two strokes of the piston, or a single crankshaft revolution.

INDEX

Photographic Credits:
t=top, b=bottom, m=middle, l=left, r=right
Cover, intro page and pages 6, 7m, 7b, 8t, 9l, 11b, 19t, 19b, 22, 25tr, 25br, 29t and back cover: Zefa; pages 7t, 9r, 26 and 28: Spectrum Colour Library; page 8: CVN Pictures; page 10: USN/DoD; pages 11t, 14r, 21l, 21r, 21m, 25tl, 27 and 29b: Robert Harding Library; pages 12, 14l, 15t and 20: Hutchison Library; page 15l: Yamaha; page 17t: Mercedes GmbH; page 17b: Quadrant Picture Library; page 18t: Vanessa Bailey; page 18: Renault UK; page 21b: NASA; page 34t: Reuter/Popperfoto; page 34l: Rex Features; page 34r: Colour-Rail.